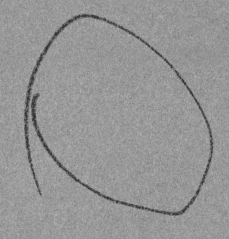

SEE THE FLY FLY

by Catherine Chase
illustrated by Bari Weissman

A DANDELION FIRST READER
VOCABULARY: 57 WORDS

DANDELION BOOKS
Published by Dandelion Press, Inc.

SEE THE FLY FLY

See the fly.
See the fly fly.

The fly flies high.
The fly flies low.

See the fly fly high.
See the fly fly low.

See where the fly goes.
The fly has landed on my nose.

The fly is flying round and round.
The fly is in a tizzy.

The fly keeps flying round and round.
That fly makes me dizzy.

See the fly.
See the fly fly.

The fly flies up.
The fly flies down.

See the fly fly up.
See the fly fly down.

See? The fly is flying by.
The fly has landed in the pie.

Oh my!
The fly is in the pie.

See the fly.
See the fly fly.

The fly flies high
Out of the pie.

The fly flies high.
The fly flies low.

It's here,
It's there,
It's everywhere!

The fly flies out.

The fly flies in.

The fly has gone into a spin.

That fly must think it is a top.
Oh! I wish that fly would <u>stop</u>.

See the fly fly.
The fly flies left.

The fly flies right.

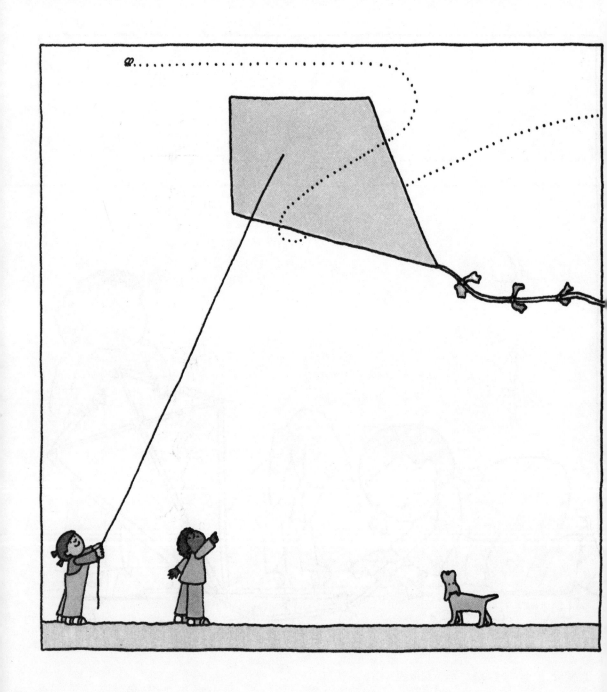

The fly flies higher than a kite.

The fly flies back.

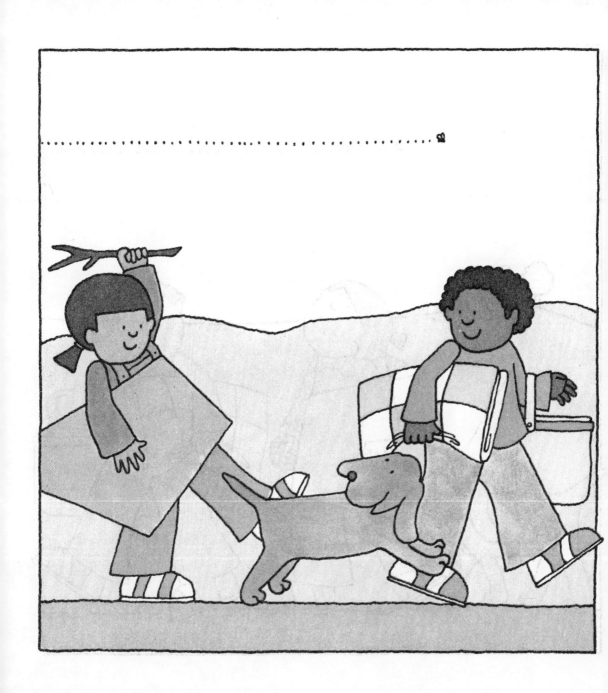

The fly flies forth.

The fly flies south.
The fly flies north.

It flies all night.

It flies all day.

I wish that fly would fly away.